OWN IT

28 DAYS TO OWN YOUR FAITH

CADE THOMPSON

Book design by Tim Murray, paperbackdesign.com/books
Text is set in Century Schoolbook, designed in 1919 by Morris Fuller Benton

Printed in the United States of America
10 9 8 7 6 5 4 3 2 1 SFP 8 19

cadethompsonmusic.com
PO Box 88004
Sioux Falls, SD 57109

HONESTLY, I could not go through life without the support of amazing people who believed in me over the years! And, to all those people I just want to say thank you!

I have to say a special thank you to Brad and Debbie for making this project possible and pouring into this mission to help change lives daily.

Thank you to my parents for being with me and supporting me since day one.

And, of course....

Thank you God for putting the vision, passion, and determination inside me so I could see this project through to the end.

CADE THOMPSON
JOSHUA 1:9

CONTENTS

INTRODUCTION

Hey, Cade here!

I'll be honest, when I first thought about writing a devotional book, it seemed like a bit of a crazy idea... But, as I've grown in my own faith walk, I've begun to understand the importance of knowing what scripture says. I want to encourage others to dig into God's word, and a devotional is a great way to do that!

What I've learned is that sometimes the best way to grow is to step out in faith and do that thing that scares you. As I saw God's plan for this book unfold, I had to ask myself, "Why *not*?"

My hope is that this devotional will encourage you and help you live out your faith no matter what your age or where you are in your faith. So... here's my challenge to you:

As you read each day's study, I hope you are motivated to stop and think about how it relates to your life, and how you can apply the scriptures.

Make that commitment, and just see what happens. I promise you, you are going to see change!

You are never too young or too old to live out what God has for you!

CADE

FOREWORD

On a hot summer day in 2015 I was introduced to 14-year-old Cade Thompson at a city-wide youth gathering. Since then, I have had the privilege of getting to know Cade as we traveled together doing ministry. I have come to know Cade as a world changer who is dedicated to serving God.

I have traveled the world doing ministry for nearly 15 years. Much of that ministry has been working with youth. One of the greatest joys in that work is getting to meet young Jesus followers from all over the world. Compared to every other meeting I have had, meeting Cade stands out!

Cade gives hope to many, and it is clear that God is doing something great through him for the next generation. God has exemplified great wisdom and maturity through Cade's life, passion, music, and now this devotional.

Cade wrote this devotional but it's clear God is the author. Through this 28-day devotional, God is speaking to the next generation in their language.

In this life God creates a beautiful masterpiece—a portrait of love we cannot fully grasp while here on this earth. But one day we will pass on and see for the first time all that God has done. It will be the lives who chose to love in the name of Jesus who will shine the brightest.

The evidence of God's masterpiece will be the words spoken, sung and written through the hearts of Jesus' followers. This book begs to be read, and I encourage all to do so. But this book must be read with the utmost respect for the truth found in its pages.

For those who follow Cade, or anyone who reads this book, I say proceed with great expectation! In this devotional you will enter into a reading of eternal significance.

This book and Cade Thompson's life are clearly pieces of that portrait. Together, they are a brush stroke in the master's hand.

I hope you enjoy reading and reflecting on the words in this book. I know you will gain a clearer picture of Jesus, the supreme example of our faith and the one behind the masterpiece.

JOSH BREWER
EVANGELIST / CEO LIFELIGHT

OWN IT

28 DAYS TO OWN YOUR FAITH

WEEK 1

GETTING STARTED

WHO IS GOD?

The word "God" is used to mean a lot of different things in our culture today. Sometimes God can seem so distant and far away—not relatable at all.

Maybe you see him as an old guy, somewhere up in the sky, holding a big hammer and just waiting for you to mess up. That belief can make us fearful of him and cause us to shy away from a relationship with him.

But God is not a heavenly bully. In fact, he's actually the opposite of that.

God is the almighty, the creator, and the designer of all things—including you and I.

COLOSSIANS 1:16 *For in him all things were created: things in heaven and on earth, visible and invisible, whether thrones or powers or rulers or authorities.*

He wants to spend time with us.

LEVITICUS 26:12 *I will walk among you and be your God, and you will be my people.*

He loves us.

1 JOHN 31:33 *See what great love the Father has lavished on us, that we should be called children of God! And that is what we are!*

And he is the hope for all mankind.

1 PETER 1:3-4 *Blessed be the God and Father of our Lord Jesus Christ! According to his great mercy, he has caused us to be born again to a living hope through the resurrection of Jesus Christ from the dead, to an inheritance that is imperishable, undefiled, and unfading, kept in heaven for you.*

He is…

God the Creator.

God the Father.

EVERLASTING FATHER

PRAYER

God, I want to know more about you. Help me understand who you are as I read your word.

CHALLENGE

Do an internet search for scriptures about who God is. Then, write down one verse that's not listed here. Give it to one person who needs to know who God is.

WHO IS JESUS?

Ever heard the saying "Like father; like son?"

Well, did you know the Bible says if you know Jesus, you know God?

JOHN 14:9 *Whoever has seen me has seen the Father.*

Jesus was fully God and fully man at the same time. He lived, walked, and breathed right here on the same earth you and I walk on.

JOHN 1:14 *And the Word became flesh and dwelt among us, and we have seen his glory, glory as of the only Son from the Father, full of grace and truth.*

Jesus was sent to save us. We all sin, but God wants every one of us to be set free. Free from past mistakes, from guilt, from shame, and free from bondage to sin.

ROMANS 3:23 *For all have sinned and fall short of the glory of God, and are justified by his grace as a gift, through the redemption that is in Christ Jesus,*

The way God accomplished that is through his son, Jesus Christ. God sent him to bridge the separation between man and God that was caused by our sin.

JOHN 3:16 *For God so loved the world, that he gave his only Son, that whoever believes in him should not perish but have eternal life.*

The Bible says that everyone who believes in Jesus will be forgiven and have everlasting life.

JOHN 3:15 *Whoever believes in him may have eternal life.*

It's so important for us understand who this man named Jesus is. He represents God's love shining down for everyone. And we know God loves us because he sent his one and only son as payment for our debt.

JOHN 1:14 *The Word became flesh and dwelt among us, and we have seen his glory, glory as of the only Son from the Father, full of grace and truth.*

PRAYER

Jesus, I ask you now to help me know you better. Show me who you are, and how to have a closer relationship with you.

CHALLENGE

Write down one of the verses above—pick the one that you were least familiar with. Put it somewhere you'll see it and read it out loud at least once a day.

WHAT DOES GOD SAY ABOUT ME?

Do you ever wonder what God thinks about you? I do!

Nobody can really know what his thoughts are, but there are many Bible verses that give a pretty good idea of what we mean to him.

The Bible says we are created in his image.

GENESIS 1:27 *God created man in his own image, in the image of God he created him; male and female he created them.*

And we are his sons and daughters.

1 JOHN 3:1 *See what kind of love the Father has given to us, that we should be called children of God; and so we are. The reason why the world does not know us is that it did not know him.*

He thinks about us a lot!

PSALM 139:17-18 *How precious to me are your thoughts, O God! How vast is the sum of them! If I would count them, they are more than the sand.*

And...

We are worth a lot to him.

MATTHEW 10:29-31 *Are not two sparrows sold for a copper coin? And not one of them falls to the ground apart from your Father's will. But the very hairs of your head are all numbered. Do not fear therefore; you are of more value than many sparrows.*

These are only a few of the Bible verses that show what God says about us. His promises for us are true, but it's up to you to choose whether or not you believe what they say.

PRAYER

Lord, help me see myself through your eyes. Help me understand how much you love me and let me walk in that every day.

CHALLENGE

Find a Bible verse that talks about how God feels about you. (Hint... remember the internet search trick?) Memorize the words (you can paraphrase!) and when you feel bad repeat your verse to yourself.

IS BEING A GOOD PERSON ENOUGH?

Most of us know people we'd describe as "good." They usually do what's right, they pretty much hang around with the right people, and they never seem to get into trouble. On the surface, they "look" decent… But what's on the outside is really all that you know about them, and looks can be deceiving.

A lot of us try to make sure what's on the outside looks good, while our insides are a mess.

I get it. See, I was raised to know what it means to be a "good person." For a long time, I thought my faith was about doing the right things. I believed it was all about making right choices – like going to youth group, not smoking, or swearing, staying out of trouble – you know… stuff like that.

But our own goodness isn't enough to save us.

ROMANS 3:23 *All have sinned and fall short of the glory of God.*

For me, everything changed when I accepted Jesus as Lord and Savior of my life. Once I made that decision, it became less about what I did, and more about my relationship with him.

PHILIPPIANS 3:8 *I count everything as loss because of the surpassing worth of knowing Christ Jesus my Lord.*

It's like this. Picture a little kid struggling to stay afloat in a pool. Imagine him struggling, but then a lifeguard dives in and pulls him out of the water. Maybe that kid thought he was a "good" swimmer.

It doesn't really matter what he believed, though – he needed a lifeguard.

PSALM 14:3 *There is none who does good—not even one.*

You know, the crazy thing is, a lifeguard is ready to jump in to help because he's there the whole time. As soon as that kid starts screaming for help – the lifeguard is right there to help. It's like that in our relationship with the Lord. He's right there the whole time. As soon as we realize we are drowning and need help, we just have to cry out and he's there.

ROMANS 10:9 *If you declare with your mouth, "Jesus is Lord," and believe in your heart that God raised him from the dead, you will be saved.*

REVELATION 3:20 *Behold, I stand at the door and knock. If anyone hears my voice and opens the door, I will come in to him and eat with him, and he with me.*

PRAYER

Heavenly Father, I call out to you. I know I can't make it on my own goodness. I see that I need to be saved and I need your help.

CHALLENGE

Make a commitment that starting today you'll take the step deeper into relationship with Jesus. In the coming weeks, use what you learn from this devotion to draw you into a closer relationship with the Lord.

WHAT IS FAITH?

What if I told you I don't believe it oxygen since I can't see or feel it? Well you might think I was crazy! We breathe it in and our bodies use it to live—whether or not we see or feel it.

We know oxygen exists despite how we physically experience it. Well, faith is very similar. It's trusting in something that we can't see, feel, or touch. It's complete trust in the middle of the unknown.

Faith is believing in God's promises and trusting in his faithfulness. It's being confident that he'll to do what he says—even when it doesn't make sense to us.

HEBREWS 11:1 *Now faith is the assurance of things hoped for, the conviction of things not seen.*

Let's be honest. Faith is easier when life is going as planned. When I feel like my life is going well, it's not hard to trust. But some days have unbelievable challenges. And when things get rough that's when it's often more difficult to have faith. But the Bible is full of stories where people had to trust, even when it was hard.

In chapter 6 of Genesis God told Noah to build an ark in the middle of a drought. It made no sense, but Noah had faith in God and obeyed.

Exodus tells the story of Moses whose parents had faith to believe that God would protect their son from a vicious pharaoh who was killing Hebrew babies. They sent him down the river in a basket.

Because of their faith, Moses survived and helped his people escape slavery.

Chapter six of Joshua tells us about the battle of Jericho. According to the story God told Joshua and his army to march around the city playing their trumpets. It may have seemed like a crazy idea, but they had faith and the walls of Jericho fell.

Faith can be big enough to move mountains, or small as a tiny mustard seed. Either way it requires a big level of trust. It may be hard for us to do, but trust like that leads to perseverance as we move through situations and see God's faithfulness.

1 CORINTHIANS 2:5 *I pray that your faith might not rest in the wisdom of men but in the power of God.*

PSALM 9:10 *Those who know your name put their trust in you, for you, O Lord, have not forsaken those who seek you.*

PSALM 56:3 *When I am afraid, I put my trust in you.*

PRAYER

Lord, help me have faith when I can't see or understand what you are doing. Show me how to trust you when it doesn't make sense to me.

CHALLENGE

Name one thing that is difficult to trust God with. Commit today to working towards having faith that he will do what he promises.

WHAT IS GRACE?

Imagine a wealthy neighbor asks you to come along on a trip around the world. It's going to be the vacation of a lifetime—the best hotels and most exciting locations. You'd love to go, but you have no way to pay for such an extravagant trip.

You're disappointed and tell him you can't go. But...

What if your neighbor generously said you could go anyway? What if the trip was yours with no expectation that you earn it or repay what it cost? It's a gift.

That's what grace is. It's a gift that's given without us deserving it, or doing anything in exchange for it. Grace is God's goodness toward those who have no claim on it, and no reason to expect it.

ROMANS 11:6 *But if it is by grace, it is no longer on the basis of works; otherwise grace would no longer be grace.*

Grace is not based on what we do, or don't do. It's something we receive when our lives are submitted to Jesus.

EPHESIANS 2:8-9 *For by grace you have been saved through faith. And this is not your own doing; it is the gift of God, not a result of works, so that no one may boast.*

It's an outrageous gift that we could never earn on our own. It leads us into repentance and forgiveness. It's the path to forgiveness and that enables us to become children of God.

JOHN 1:16 *And from his fullness we have all received, grace upon grace.*

PRAYER
Lord, let me see the many ways you've blessed my life in ways I did not deserve. Show me the way to forgiveness through your gift of grace.

CHALLENGE
Reflect on the many ways God has shown grace in your life. Write them down inside your Bible or journal. Answer this question: "What is one-way God's grace drawn me to him?

WHAT IS MERCY?

Imagine a man on death row. As he faces the end of his life, he knows he deserves the penalty he's about to pay. At the last minute – moments before he's to be executed, he is set free because someone else agrees to take the penalty in his place. Not only is he not going to die, he's going to live as a free man. He will never have to pay for what he did because someone else paid it for him.

That is mercy.

Mercy is demonstrated through God's complete and loving compassion. He loves us so much that he sent Jesus to pay the penalty for our sins, and Jesus willingly paid our debt because.

The amazing thing is, that God did that despite everything we've done—or will do in the future. Through mercy we are fully pardoned for our sins and failures even though we don't deserve it and can't earn it.

JAMES 2:13 *For judgment is without mercy to one who has shown no mercy. Mercy triumphs over judgment.*

HEBREWS 4:16 *Let us then with confidence draw near to the throne of grace, that we may receive mercy and find grace to help in time of need.*

As human beings we are all messy. Every one of us sins, but despite our failures God desires to have a relationship with us.

TITUS 3:5 *He saved us, not because of works done by us in righteousness, but according to his own mercy.*

He pours out mercy.

LAMENTATIONS 3:22-23 *The steadfast love of the Lord never ceases; his mercies never come to an end; they are new every morning; great is your faithfulness.*

PRAYER

Heavenly Father, thank you for showing me mercy when I didn't deserve it. I pray you'd help me remember the great gift you gave through your son, Jesus.

CHALLENGE

Reflect on the mistakes and failures in your life. Then, write down three examples of God's mercy.

WEEK 2

GOING DEEPER

HOW DO WE HAVE JOY IN ALL CIRCUMSTANCES?

No one walks through life without experiencing both happy and sad feelings. But, do you ever feel like your emotions are as unreliable as the weather?

Think about how you feel when you're having a good day. Everything's going your way and all seems right with the world. Sure, it's easy to feel happiness on those days. But how does it feel when everything seems to go south?

JOHN 16:33 *I have said these things to you, that in me you may have peace. In the world you will have tribulation. But take heart; I have overcome the world.*

The Bible says we should always be joyful.

PHILIPPIANS 4:4 *Rejoice in the Lord always; again, I will say, Rejoice.*

How's that even possible?

Well, first we need to stop confusing joy with happiness. They are two different things.

You see, happiness is based on what's going on around us. Most of the time, happy feelings are temporary because things can change in a moment's notice.

Joy is something different. According to God's word we can experience joy when things are not going well.

JAMES 1:2-4 *Count it all joy, my brothers, when you meet trials of various kinds, for you know that the testing of your faith produces steadfastness. And let steadfastness have its full effect, that you may be perfect and complete, lacking in nothing.*

That's because joy is not based on our circumstances. It comes right from the Lord. It's about where we focus.

DEUTERONOMY 31:6 *Be strong and courageous. Do not fear or be in dread of them, for it is the LORD your God who goes with you. He will not leave you or forsake you.*

When our eyes are set on the things of heaven and not on the temporary, we find JOY.

JOHN 16:22 *So also you have sorrow now, but I will see you again, and your hearts will rejoice, and no one will take your joy from you.*

PSALM 16:11 *You make known to me the path of life; in your presence there is fullness of joy; at your right hand are pleasures forevermore.*

CHOOSE JOY EVERLASTING

PRAYER

Lord, help me see you in the middle of the hard stuff. Let me know you are with me every step of every day. Show me how to have joy every day.

CHALLENGE

Write down one of the scriptures listed above—or find your own. Put it somewhere that's easy to get to. Next time you have a difficult day, go find that scripture and read it out loud.

WHAT ARE GOD'S PROMISES FOR ME?

Have you ever made a promise you didn't keep? Or, has someone promised you something only to fail to follow through with it?

Yeah, we've all probably been on both sides of that situation. As humans we aren't always good at keeping promises.

But God is not like that—his promises can be counted on.

2 CORINTHIANS 1:20 *For all the promises of God find their Yes and amen in him.*

2 PETER 1:4 *He has given us his very great and precious promises.*

The Bible is full of God's promises. There are...

Promises for safety and protection:

ISAIAH 54:17 *No weapon that is fashioned against you shall succeed.*

PSALM 46:1 *God is our refuge and strength, a very present help in trouble.*

Promises that he loves and saves us:

JOHN 3:16 *For God so loved the world, that he gave his only Son, that whoever believes in him should not perish but have eternal life.*

Promises about our future:

JEREMIAH 29:11 *For I know the plans I have for you, declares the Lord, plans for welfare and not for evil,* *to give you a future and a hope.*

There are promises for literally every situation in your life. And they are trustworthy because God doesn't shift or change. He's true and good and what he promises is true and good.

JAMES 1:17 *Every good gift and every perfect gift is from above, coming down from the Father of lights, with whom there is no variation or shadow due to change.*

But God's promises don't necessarily mean an easy or struggle free life. As a matter of fact, in our world today there's a good chance you'll have hard things happen. But, no matter, it doesn't change God's promises for you.

NUMBERS 23:19 *God is not man, that he should lie, or a son of man, that he should change his mind. Has he said, and will he not do it? Or has he spoken, and will he not fulfill it?*

PRAYER

Lord, show me who you are through your promises for me. Let me learn what YOU say about me and your plans for me.

CHALLENGE

Find at least 5 promises that you can relate to. Make a list and put them in your Bible or on your refrigerator. Read one out loud each day for the next 5 days.

ARE GOD'S PROMISES TRUE FOR ME?

The world is not perfect. Every day, we experience things that can make us less trusting. Sometimes we find out people are not who they portray themselves to be. Or, we learn about how unreliable our friends can be.

These experiences can cause us to mistrust. And that can make us doubt what God says and question if his promises are true for us.

But remember what we learned about God's promises being true?

2 CORINTHIANS 1:20 *For all the promises of God find their Yes and amen in him.*

And...

NUMBERS 23:19 *Has God said it, and will he not do it? Or has he spoken, and will he not fulfill it?*

God is not a liar. I can tell you over and over that God's promises are very true, but ultimately you choose if you are going to believe what he says or not.

The thing is, sometimes we get disappointed because we don't get something we prayed for. God's promises don't mean getting what we want every time.

Even if we don't get everything we want, God's promises are true.

2 TIMOTHY 3:16 *All Scripture is breathed out by God and profitable for teaching, for reproof, for correction, and for training in righteousness,*

God is sovereign, and sometimes his plan for our lives look different than we expect. But remember, he sees the big picture and we do not. Even when he says "no," or "not right now," it doesn't change the fact that what he promises is true.

ROMANS 8:28 *And we know that for those who love God all things work together for good, for those who are called according to his purpose.*

PRAYER
Lord, help me when I don't believe your promises. Show me how to believe, even when it doesn't match up with what I think should happen.

CHALLENGE
Write down one promise that you KNOW is true. Reflect on how God's promise impacts your life.

WHAT DOES GOD SAY ABOUT SIN?

Many times, we describe sin using words like "mistake," or "failure," or even an "oops." No matter what you call it, sin is anything that separates us from God.

The Bible says that God is Holy and there is no sin in him.

1 JOHN 1:5 *This is the message we have heard from him and proclaim to you, that God is light, and in him is no darkness at all.*

But the Bible also says we have all sinned.

ROMANS 3:23-24 *For all have sinned and fall short of the glory of God, and are justified by his grace as a gift, through the redemption that is in Christ Jesus.*

Every one of us comes into this world with a sin nature. That means we are capable of failing in what we do, what we say, or even what we think. If what we do goes against what God says, it's sin.

But we are still able to have a relationship with God because Jesus paid the price for our failure. Because of him, we have access to God.

ACTS 4:12 *And there is salvation in no one else, for there is no other name under heaven given among men by which we must be saved.*

When we come into relationship with God our mindset changes. Through our relationship with him, we grow to realize the power of striving for a holy lifestyle.

ROMANS 12:2 *Do not be conformed to this world, but be transformed by the renewal of your mind, that by testing you may discern what is the will of God, what is good and acceptable and perfect.*

But we've got to be honest with ourselves and God about what's going on.

1 JOHN 1:9 *If we confess our sins, he is faithful and just to forgive us our sins and to cleanse us from all unrighteousness.*

Through Christ our relationship with God is restored, and sin is covered.

AMOS 9:14 *I will restore my people.*

1 JOHN 5:4 *for everyone born of God overcomes the world. This is the victory that has overcome the world, even our faith.*

PRAYER

Lord, help me see where I've fallen short and sinned. Show me what ways I'm failing to live a holy life.

CHALLENGE

Reflect on the last few days. Can you see one or two ways you've sinned? Be honest with yourself and God. Ask him to forgive you.

WHAT DOES IT MEAN TO REPENT?

Have you ever known someone who continually says they are sorry, but keeps doing the thing they apologize for? What if they never changed that behavior? It would be frustrating, right?

But what if they realized what they were doing, asked you to forgive them, AND changed their behavior?

Well, it's a bit like that when we repent. It's not just about just admitting what we did and saying we're sorry,

1 JOHN 1:9 *If we confess our sins, he is faithful and just and will forgive us our sins and purify us from all unrighteousness.*

We also have to turn around our behavior.

ACTS 3:19 *Repent therefore, and turn back, that your sins may be blotted out.*

God wants us to change our minds, and go in the opposite direction. But sometimes it seems like the hardest thing we ever have to do. As humans, we often struggle with admitting we are wrong. The good news is we have help there too, because God's love leads us to repentance.

ROMANS 2:4 *Or do you presume on the riches of his kindness and forbearance and patience, not knowing that God's kindness is meant to lead you to repentance?*

True repentance happens when we begin to see things as God sees them. It's a heart shift. It's about turning around and walking in a different direction.

PSALM 51:10-12 *Create in me a pure heart, O God, and renew a steadfast spirit within me. Do not cast me from your presence or take your Holy Spirit from me. Restore to me the joy of your salvation and grant me a willing spirit, to sustain me.*

PRAYER

Lord, just like David in Psalms, I ask you to make my heart clean. Show me where I need to repent, and give me strength to do so.

CHALLENGE

Identify one area in your life where you know God is calling you to repent. First pray and ask him to forgive you. Then, commit to changing that behavior for good.

WHAT IS LIVING A LIFE OF GRATEFULNESS?

Imagine you got your best friend a gift. You spent weeks planning what to get. You spent a fair amount of money. And, you got something you knew was something they really wanted and needed.

The big day comes. The gift is unwrapped, and it's hard to miss the eye-roll and unmistakable look of disappointment. How would that feel?

Wow. That may seem like a silly example, but sometimes that's how we are with the gifts God gives. We have breath, and life, and sun, and love, and flowers, and… You name it. But instead of being grateful, all we can think about is the one thing we didn't get.

We often focus so much on what's not right that we miss the incredible blessings we receive every day. But that kind of attitude is no small thing.

PHILIPPIANS 2:14 *Do all things without grumbling.*

EXODUS 16:8 *You are not grumbling against us, but against the LORD*

Living a life of gratitude means shifting our eyes off ourselves. In today's world we are taught to focus on "ME." But, God tells us the opposite.

PHILIPPIANS 2:3-4 *Do nothing from rivalry or conceit, but in humility count others more significant than yourselves. Let each of you look not only to his own interests, but also to the interests of others.*

As much as it can be hard to swallow that thought, it is very true. If you want to know how to do that, Jesus is your example. He lived that out every day.

PHILIPPIANS 2:6-7 *Who, being in very nature God, did not consider equality with God something to be used to his own advantage; rather, he made himself nothing by taking the very nature of a servant, being made in human likeness.*

Be grateful for all that God has done for you—in the good times and bad. Remember what you've been given in the poor times and abundantly rich times.

HAVE A HEART SHIFT

PRAYER
Lord, forgive me for taking your gifts for granted. Help me to remember the extravagant blessing of your love.

CHALLENGE
Write down 10 things you are grateful for. Post it somewhere you can see it.

DO MY THOUGHTS MATTER?

There's an old Sunday school song written for little kids that talks about being careful what you think. It may be a kindergarten song, but it's got a lot of truth to it. Besides, it must matter what we think because the Bible says a lot about our minds and what we think.

It says to guard our mind (heart).

PROVERBS 4:23 *Keep your heart with all vigilance, for from it flow the springs of life.*

And, that renewing our mind can change us:

ROMANS 12:2 *Do not conform to the pattern of this world, but be transformed by the renewing of your mind.*

But I get it. We can try to be careful about what we watch on TV or in the movies. We can listen to Christian music or read only Christian authors. But if we live in this world, soon or later, we're going to be exposed to things that are not good for us.

You can't always control what comes into your mind. What matters is what you do with those thoughts. You have control over whether or not you let those thoughts take hold. If you have thoughts that you KNOW are not right, by all means don't keep rolling it around in your head!

Here's how you do that. Use scripture, music, and prayer to change what you're thinking.

2 CORINTHIANS 10:4-6 *We destroy arguments and every lofty opinion raised against the knowledge of God, and take every thought captive to obey Christ, being ready to punish every disobedience, when your obedience is complete.*

Keep your eyes are situationally focused. Pay attention to what you pay attention to. Think through the lens of JESUS.

Think about GOOD things:

PHILIPPIANS 4:8 *Finally, brothers, whatever is true, whatever is honorable, whatever is just, whatever is pure, whatever is lovely, whatever is commendable, if there is any excellence, if there is anything worthy of praise, think about these things.*

Focus on GOD:

ISAIAH 26:3 *You keep him in perfect peace whose mind is stayed on you,*

Remember we have HIS mind:

PHILIPPIANS 2:5 *Have this mind among yourselves, which is yours in Christ Jesus.*

PRAYER

Lord, help me pay attention to what I think about. When I find myself thinking about things, I shouldn't help me turn to you for help.

CHALLENGE

Identify and memorize ONE scripture that you can use when you are tempted to think about things you shouldn't.

MAKING IT PERSONAL

I'M A CHRISTIAN—NOW WHAT?

No matter how old you are your life experiences are made up of good and bad, and big and small events.

Sometimes though experiences are life-changing. That's what being born again was like for me. It's one of the most impactful experiences I've ever had, and it changed me.

There are so many things that happen when we become Christians. For one, the Bible says when we are saved, we become God's children, and receive eternal life.

JOHN 1:12 *But to all who did receive him, who believed in his name, he gave the right to become children of God.*

JOHN 5:24 *Truly, truly, I say to you, whoever hears my word and believes him who sent me has eternal life.*

But salvation isn't just about what we get. It should cause us to see people differently, and it should change how we interact with those around us.

Here's how.

Take a look at Matthew chapter 22. In this story, someone asks Jesus what the greatest commandment is. Now this guy was trying to trick Jesus into saying something that would get him into trouble. But Jesus' answer is a big clue to what our lives should look like.

Here's how Jesus responded:

MATTHEW 22:37-39 *"You shall love the Lord your God with all your heart and with all your soul and with all your mind. This is the great and first commandment. And a second is like it: You shall love your neighbor as yourself.*

So, to me, the greatest change in our lives should be how we love God and others. It comes down to this: everything we do—from relationships to work to play to worship displays our love for God.

1 PETER 3:8 *Finally, all of you, have unity of mind, sympathy, brotherly love, a tender heart, and a humble mind.*

1 JOHN 3:11 *For this is the message that you have heard from the beginning, that we should love one another.*

And....

JOHN 13:34, 35 *A new commandment I give to you, that you love one another: just as I have loved you, you also are to love one another. By this all people will know that you are my disciples, if you have love for one another.*

PRAYER
Heavenly Father, help me love you with my whole heart, and help me love others the way you would.

CHALLENGE
Think of one person you don't usually hang out with or talk to. Make a point of saying hi to them. If possible, reach out today through text or social media and tell them you are thinking of them.

WHAT IS MY TRUE IDENTITY?

Identity describes who we are. It includes everything that makes us unique, and includes things like the way we look, talk, laugh, and walk, and the things we like or dislike. It's how the world sees us.

The Bible says we are uniquely made.

PSALM 139:14 *I praise you, for I am fearfully and wonderfully made. Wonderful are your works; my soul knows it very well.*

And set apart.

JEREMIAH 1:5 *Before I formed you in the womb, I knew you, and before you were born, I consecrated you;*

God created us for a purpose he designed for us.

1 PETER 4:10-11 *As each has received a gift, use it to serve one another, as good stewards of God's varied grace:*

The thing is, our identity is tied to God's purpose for us, and that's important.

COLOSSIANS 3:17 *And whatever you do, in word or deed, do everything in the name of the Lord Jesus, giving thanks to God the Father through him.*

One thing is clear though, our purpose and identity are not to be used for our own selfish ambitions.

PHILIPPIANS 2:3-4 *Do nothing from rivalry or conceit, but in humility count others more significant than yourselves. Let each of you look not only to his own interests, but also to the interests of others.*

What we do every day, should show others who he is.

EPHESIANS 5:1 *Therefore be imitators of God, as beloved children.*

1 TIMOTHY 4:12 *Let no one despise you for your youth, but set the believers an example in speech, in conduct, in love, in faith, in purity.*

PRAYER

Lord, show me my true identity. Teach me how to draw others to Christ through the way I live.

CHALLENGE

Take an honest look at your lifestyle. Name one thing that does not truly represent your relationship with God. Write down how you will change that behavior.

WHAT DOES IT MEAN TO BE THE LIGHT?

The gospel is the story of Good news of Jesus. Understanding our part in that good news story is an important part of our lives as believers.

Living out the Gospel is all about relationship not religion. And that relationship begins with us.

We are called to share this good news with the world.

ROMANS 5:15 *But the free gift is not like the transgression. For if by the transgression of the one the many died, much more did the grace of God and the gift by the grace of the one Man, Jesus Christ, abound to the many.*

The Gospel is about an incredible gift that's available. Think about it—if you were excited about a gift, you'd been given I bet you wouldn't hesitate to tell everyone about it.

ACTS 13:47 *For so the Lord has commanded us, saying, "I have made you a light for the Gentiles, that you may bring salvation to the ends of the earth."*

LUKE 8:16 *[Jesus said,] "No one after lighting a lamp covers it with a jar or puts it under a bed, but puts it on a stand, so that those who enter may see the light."*

We are called to be a light to others and the light we shine should draw others to Jesus.

MATTHEW 5:14-16 *[Jesus said,] "You are the light of the world. Let your light shine before others, so that they may see your good works and give glory to your Father who is in heaven.*

EPHESIANS 5:8 *For at one time you were darkness, but now you are light in the Lord. Walk as children of light.*

PRAYER

Lord, show me how to be a light in a dark world. Teach me how to draw others to Christ through the way I live.

CHALLENGE

Write down one thing you can do to "shine" for Jesus. Commit to meeting that goal within the next month.

WHAT IF LIFE GETS HARD?

Everyone has good and bad days, but have you ever just simply hit rock bottom?

Sometimes there are moments it can feel like we are lost in a hot dry desert with no water and no shade.

Maybe you've even felt like giving up on life all together? If you are there, let me encourage you.

YOUR STORY IS FAR FROM OVER

No situation is too big for God, and we can never be too far for his hand to save us.

PSALM 73:23, 24 *Nevertheless, I am continually with you; you hold my right hand. You guide me with your counsel, and afterward you will receive me to glory.*

The things we go through are sometimes seem like they will destroy us, but God can use what we experience for GOOD.

GENESIS 50:20 *As for you, you meant evil against me, but God meant it for good,*

Scriptures tell us to take up your cross and follow JESUS. That means we need to keep walking. Everyone goes through tough things, but the trick is to never give up.

MATTHEW 16:24-26 *Then Jesus told his disciples, "If anyone would come after me, let him deny himself and take up his cross and follow me."*

Look up and keep focused on the one who can take you through the desert places in your life.

ISAIAH 43:19 *Behold, I am doing a new thing; now it springs forth, do you not perceive it? I will make a way in the wilderness and rivers in the desert.*

JEREMIAH 31:25 *For I will satisfy the weary soul, and every languishing soul I will replenish.*

PRAYER

Lord, when I feel like I'm lost in a desert remind me that you are always there to refresh me. Help me run to you.

CHALLENGE

Find and write down one scripture you can read when you find yourself in a desert place. Put it in your Bible or somewhere you can find it when you need it.

DO I HAVE TO READ THE BIBLE?

The older I get, the more I am reminded of how powerful it is to dig into the TRUE word of GOD.

His WORD is LIFE. It is like water and food for our soul.

Most of us wouldn't think of going too many days without food. Well, it should be the same with the Bible. We need God's word every day.

MATTHEW 6:11 *Give us this day our daily bread...*

It's God's direction for our lives.

2 TIMOTHY 3:16,17 *All Scripture is breathed out by God and profitable for teaching, for reproof, for correction, and for training in righteousness, that the man of God may be complete, equipped for every good work.*

God's word is forever.

MATTHEW 24:35 *Heaven and earth will pass away, but my words will not pass away.*

It's alive, relevant to our lives, and powerful.

HEBREWS 4:12 *For the word of God is living and active, sharper than any two-edged sword.*

The Bible provides instruction that teaches us how to live as Christians. It's full of astonishing and extraordinary promises that belong to us. Scripture our lifeblood.

PRAYER
Lord, give me a desire for your word. Help me make studying scripture a priority.

CHALLENGE
Commit to reading at least ONE verse per day for the next seven days. (Hint: there are many Bible apps that will send a verse to your cell phone daily.)

WHAT'S THE RIGHT AGE TO SERVE GOD?

Have you had anyone say you couldn't do something because you were too old or too young?

Age should not matter. The truth is whether you are 5 or 85, sometimes we are judged because of our age. But did you know the Bible calls us to be the example no matter what our age is?

1 TIMOTHY 4:12 *Let no one despise you for your youth, but set the believers an example in speech, in conduct, in love, in faith, in purity.*

In our culture there's a perception that age plays a part in the gifts and passions the Lord gives us. But the Bible is full of stories where people of all ages accomplished great things for God.

David was only 17 when he killed Goliath.

2 SAMUEL 17:50 *So David prevailed over the Philistine with a sling and with a stone, and struck the Philistine and killed him.*

And Moses was 80 when he was called to set his people free.

EXODUS 3:10 *Come, I will send you to Pharaoh that you may bring my people, the children of Israel, out of Egypt.*

The Bible says everyone is called to serve. And serving God is a lifetime commitment. Don't second guess yourself because of your age. You're never too old or young to follow Jesus' example.

MARK 10:45 *For even the Son of Man came not to be served but to serve, and to give his life as a ransom for many.*

PRAYER

Lord, thank you that I can serve you today, whatever my age. I ask you to show me how and where I need to serve.

CHALLENGE

Do one thing for someone else today. If you can, try to do it anonymously.

WHAT IS A SURRENDERED LIFE?

When we surrender to God, we completely give up our own will, thoughts, ideas, and deeds to God. It means accepting his will for us.

We are called to surrender. But to be honest, sometimes it's very hard to do.

There are so many things competing to distract us from the life that God calls us to. Like me you may find that life gets in the way of real surrender. Do you worry that it means giving up everything as you know it and moving to a hut in a desert where you live off grasshoppers?

Okay maybe that's a bit dramatic. But truthfully, surrender is not about a life without. It's about a life WITH.

It's about living your life guided and directed by the Lord.

PROVERBS 16:3 *Commit your work to the Lord, and your plans will be established.*

PROVERBS 23:26 *My son, give me your heart, and let your eyes observe my ways.*

When we become Christians, the life we live is no longer ours—it belongs to him.

GALATIANS 2:20 *I have been crucified with Christ. It is no longer I who live, but Christ who lives in me. And the life I now live in the flesh I live by faith in the Son of God, who loved me and gave himself for me.*

Surrender simply means he becomes the Lord and the ruler of your life.

ROMANS 12:1,2 *I appeal to you therefore, brothers, by the mercies of God, to present your bodies as a living sacrifice, holy and acceptable to God, which is your spiritual worship.*

PRAYER
Lord, help me surrender daily to you. Show me how to make you Lord of my life.

CHALLENGE
Commit to one part of your life you need to surrender to God. Write it down and post it somewhere you'll see it every day.

WEEK 4

WEEK 4

OWNING YOUR FAITH

WHAT ARE THE DESIRES OF MY HEART?

Every human being has hopes and dreams. Everyone has something they want to do or experience.

When we come into relationship with God, I believe the desires of our hearts begins to align with God's desires for our lives. What we want is directly related to our relationship with Christ.

You see, God created us with specific gifts and talents to be used for a purpose he designed just for us.

EPHESIANS 1:11 *In him we have obtained an inheritance, having been predestined according to the purpose of him who works all things according to the counsel of his will.*

That's how it was for me. When I came to know JESUS as my savior, I had things I wanted to do. What I found was that as I focused on HIM, I started to see the Lord bring those desires into focus.

MATTHEW 7:7, 8 *Ask, and it will be given to you; seek, and you will find; knock, and it will be opened to you. For everyone who asks receives, and the one who seeks finds, and to the one who knocks it will be opened.*

The Bible says we need to seek HIM first.

JEREMIAH 29:13 *You will seek me and find me, when you seek me with all your heart.*

PRAYER

Heavenly Father, I ask you to help me realize the desire of my heart. Help me put you first and seek you in all I do.

CHALLENGE

Write down one or two "desires of your heart." Put them somewhere you will see them every day—like the bathroom mirror. Then pray and ask God.

WHAT IS MY PURPOSE?

Our purpose involves something greater than ourselves... that is the big thing about that says "You exist to bring GOD GLORY."

After I began to grow closer to the Lord, he began to reveal my purpose through his spirit of wisdom and revelation upon me.

Proverbs 16:1 The plans of the heart belong to man, but the answer of the tongue is from the Lord.

The best way to figure out YOUR purpose is to dig into God's word!

ASK

SEEK

KNOCK

MATTHEW 6:33 *But seek first the kingdom of God and his righteousness, and all these things will be added to you.*

I encourage you to focus on your relationship with the Lord—first and foremost. Then begin to ask him to show you what YOUR purpose is. I bet when you do, you'll see how much his purpose aligns with the desires of YOUR heart.

EXODUS 9:16 *But for this purpose I have raised you up, to show you my power, so that my name may be proclaimed in all the earth.*

PSALM 37:4 *Delight yourself in the Lord, and he will give you the desires of your heart.*

PRAYER
Lord, help me to seek you in everything I do. Show me what your purpose is for my life.

CHALLENGE
Look for three scriptures about purpose. Write them in the back of your Bible. Set a reminder on your phone to read them once a week.

HOW DO I TURN FEAR INTO FAITH?

Have you ever found yourself lying in bed looking at the ceiling and worrying about the future? Maybe you're stressed over school, relationships, family, work... Whatever.

The thing is, you're in good company if you answered "yes" to the question. But as Christians we are supposed to 'cast our cares" on the Lord.

The Bible says that even the ravens do not worry about what they will eat or drink, so why should we?

LUKE 12:24 *Consider the ravens: they neither sow nor reap, they have neither storehouse nor barn, and yet God feeds them. Of how much more value are you than the birds!*

I get that life isn't always easy. Sometimes we go through many transitions, life changing moments, and shifting seasons of life. All of that can make us feel uneasy or anxious.

JOHN 16:33 *I have said these things to you, that in me you may have peace. In the world you will have tribulation. But take heart; I have overcome the world.*

JOB 5:7 *For man is born for trouble.*

But if we set our hope on Christ alone, we find peace in the middle of trouble. It may not make sense in our human minds, but it's God's promise to us.

PHILIPPIANS 4:7 *And the peace of God, which surpasses all understanding, will guard your hearts and your minds in Christ Jesus.*

Faith over fear demands that we trust... If you find yourself wallowing in anxiousness and worry, maybe you are living in a spirit of fear INSTEAD OF Faith. Remember that even the longest nights are always followed by morning.

1 PETER 5:7 *Casting all your anxieties on him, because he cares for you.*

Ask God to help you turn...

FEAR INTO FAITH.

PRAYER
Lord, I right now I confess my fear and lay it at the foot of the cross. Help me to have faith in the night—even when I can't see the dawn.

CHALLENGE
Write down one fear that you are committed to surrendering to God. Ask him to help you change that fear into faith. Then, burn or shred what you wrote down.

HOW DO I SHARE MY FAITH?

Let's just be honest here. Sometimes sharing our faith can be awkward. In today's world where people are so sensitive about so many topics, it can even feel a bit taboo.

Sharing my faith can sometimes be a struggle for me, and I know it is for some of you too. So how do we get past this?

First of all, we are supposed to share our faith with others. The Bible clearly shows this is something we should be doing.

MATTHEW 28:19 *Go therefore and make disciples of all nations, baptizing them in the name of the Father and of the Son and of the Holy Spirit.*

And it's not about having all the right answers because the Bible says God will help us know what to say.

MATTHEW 10:19 *So not be anxious how you are to speak or what you are to say, for what you are to say will be given to you in that hour.*

And,

EXODUS 4:12 *Now therefore go, and I will be with your mouth and teach you what you shall speak.*

I believe it starts with the relationships we establish with others. Jesus focused on people, and so should we.

MATTHEW 25:40 *Truly, I say to you, as you did it to one of the least of these my brothers, you did it to me.*

When we care about people, we demonstrate how Jesus feels about them. He wants a relationship with them—just like he does with us. And through these relationships people can see the true hope inside us.

MATTHEW 5:16 *In the same way, let your light shine before others, so that they may see your good works and give glory to your Father who is in heaven.*

Yes, it may mean talking to someone you usually wouldn't. And it may feel weird at first. But remember, you are sharing really good news.

JOHN 3:16 *For God so loved the world, that he gave his only Son, that whoever believes in him should not perish but have eternal life.*

PRAYER

God help me to love people the way you do. Give me the right words to say so I can tell them the good news about your love for the.

CHALLENGE

Pray and ask the Lord to reveal a specific person you can share this gift with. Make a point of reaching out to that person and inviting them to lunch or coffee.

HOW DO I PARTICIPATE IN THE GOSPEL?

Have you ever been to a sporting event where every one of the players sat on the sidelines the entire game? That would be ridiculous. What good would it do if everyone was on the bench, and no one actually played in the game?

Well, that's how it would look if every Christian decided it was someone else's job to lead. Look, God has called every one of us to step into the game of life. We participate in the Gospel when we commit to serving others.

We are called to lead by example in our faith, in relationships, in our jobs, in our communities, and to everyone we come in contact with. We are to serve through the gifts God gave us.

1 PETER 4:10 *As each has received a gift, use it to serve one another, as good stewards of God's varied grace.*

1 JOHN 3:18 *Let us not love in word or talk but in deed and in truth.*

Giving, leading, and serving are the living standards that God has called us to.

HEBREWS 13:16 *Do not neglect to do good and to share what you have, for such sacrifices are pleasing to God.*

GALATIANS 6:9 *And let us not grow weary of doing good, for in due season we will reap, if we do not give up.*

PHILIPPIANS 2:4 *Let each of you look not only to his own interests, but also to the interests of others.*

As Christians we are equipped to serve. It's not just what we do – it's who we are.

JAMES 2:14-17 *What good is it, my brothers, if someone says he has faith but does not have works? Can that faith save him? If a brother or sister is poorly clothed and lacking in daily food, and one of you says to them, "Go in peace, be warmed and filled," without giving them the things needed for the body, what good is that? So also, faith by itself, if it does not have works, is dead.*

PRAYER

Lord, help me see the need around me and give me a heart to serve. Show me where I can help people.

CHALLENGE

Identify one place you can serve – whether in church, at school, or in the community. Commit to volunteering at least once in the next week.

HOW DO I KNOW I CAN SHARE MY FAITH?

We've already established that as Christians we are called to share the gospel with others. It's a charge every believer has been tasked with.

But, look, I get it. It's one thing to understand the Gospel for myself, and another to feel like I have what it takes to own it enough to share with others.

1 TIMOTHY 6:12 *Fight the good fight of the faith. Take hold of the eternal life to which you were called and about which you made the good confession in the presence of many witnesses.*

It can seem impossible, but the Bible says we are equipped in our faith to do God's will and to share the good news with others.

HEBREWS 13:21 *He equips you with everything good that you may do his will, working in us that which is pleasing in his sight, through Jesus Christ, to whom be glory forever and ever.*

That means it doesn't matter if we feel we have what we need to share the Gospel with others. God HAS supplied us with what we need to do that work.

2 PETER 1:3 *His divine power has granted to us all things that pertain to life and godliness, through the knowledge of him who called us to his own glory and excellence,*

Look, there will always be people who come against your beliefs. They will question what God's word says. But don't worry! You don't have to convince them. Your job is to stand firm.

EPHESIANS 6:13 .... *having done all, stand firm.*

Because....

2 CORINTHIANS 10:3 *For though we walk in the flesh, we are not waging war according to the flesh. For the weapons of our warfare are not of the flesh but have divine power to destroy strongholds. We destroy arguments and every lofty opinion raised against the knowledge of God, and take every thought captive to obey Christ,*

So, go ahead and share your faith. Then, stand firm in him alone. All other ground is sinking sand.

NO COMPROMISE

PRAYER

Lord, equip me to share my faith with others. Help me to stand firm in what I know about you and your saving grace.

CHALLENGE

Commit today to sharing your faith with ONE person before the end of the week.

WHAT DOES OWNING MY FAITH MEAN?

Before you were born God created you—uniquely for a purpose he designed for you before you came to be.

JEREMIAH 1:5 *Before I formed you in the womb, I knew you, and before you were born, I consecrated you;*

Every day you have a choice to walk in what you were created to be, or to run away and find your own way. It's a choice we are all faced with. Free will means that we get to decide. You determine how you choose, think, and act

PROVERBS 16:9 *The heart of man plans his way.*

JOSHUA 24:15 *Choose this day whom you will serve.*

Living your story really is about being sold out for God. It's a life in full submission him. Scary as that may sound to you, it's the highest and best way to live. That's what I've learned, and I pray that for you we well.

PSALM 37:23 *The steps of a man are established by the Lord, when he delights in his way;*

2 TIMOTHY 1:9 *God saved us and called us to a holy calling, not because of our works but because of his own purpose and grace, which he gave us in Christ Jesus before the ages began,*

It's not difficult. It happens when our eyes turn off of ourselves and look at Jesus square in the face.

MATTHEW 6:33 *But seek first the kingdom of God and his righteousness, and all these things will be added to you.*

PROVERBS 3:5-6 *Trust in the Lord with all your heart, and do not lean on your own understanding. In all your ways acknowledge him, and he will make straight your paths.*

Then just like a mirror our lives can start to reflect all that GOD has for us. This means sharing the GOSPEL, and living a

GOSPEL CENTERED LIFE.

PRAYER

Dear God, help me to be wholly sold out to you. Show me what it means to live the story you created for me.

CHALLENGE

Begin today to seek God's purpose in your life. Ask him to unfold the story he designed for you.

OWN IT

CONTINUE ON YOUR JOURNEY

I hope this devotional inspired you to dig deep and to own your faith walk. Living your faith takes courage!

Change can happen no matter where you are in your personal journey. But it doesn't happen unless you stay committed to the process. No one can do this for you.

Owning your Faith is a life-long process. Here are a few things you can do to continue what you've started:

- Read scripture daily! Reading God's word will change your life, so make reading the Bible a habit!

- Re-read the devotional! Change takes repetition, and this study is meant to be repeated.

- If you completed the devotional on your own, think about finding a few friends to go through it with you. Encourage and help others with what you've learned.

- Get into (or start) a small group and dig into scripture. Make commitments to challenge your faith, and hold each other accountable.

Small commitments can have life-changing impact. Remember... You are never too young or too old to live out what God has for you! Now go...

OWN IT!

ABOUT THE AUTHOR

Cade Thompson is a contemporary Christian music artist whose sound appeals to a wide audience.

His music combines faith with powerful melodies and lyrics. Cade's relatable music inspires and encourages listeners to explore and deepen their faith in tangible ways.

'Faithful and True' was Cade's first single, and was written and recorded at age fourteen. Today, Cade continues to reveal his heart for God through music. Songs such as Voices, Almost Dawn, Grateful, Treasures, Lights, and To Really Be Alive give voice to the experiences of any generation.

Cade's music is available on all streaming platforms, and you can catch him live at concerts and festivals.

FOLLOW:
INSTAGRAM: @cadethompsonmusic
FACEBOOK: @cadethompsonmusic
TWITTER: @cade_thompson_
CONTACT: cadethompsonmusic.com